MIGHTY MACHINES

Written by Rupert Matthews

Illustrated by Sebastian Quigley

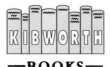
KIBWORTH
—BOOKS—

Bulldozer

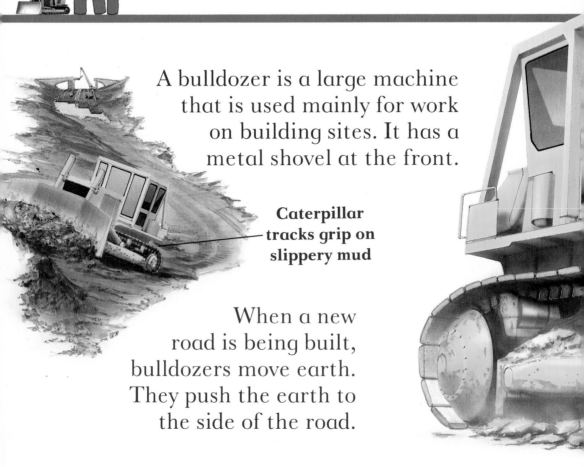

A bulldozer is a large machine that is used mainly for work on building sites. It has a metal shovel at the front.

Caterpillar tracks grip on slippery mud

When a new road is being built, bulldozers move earth. They push the earth to the side of the road.

Roller

Sometimes a bulldozer pulls a roller. This flattens the earth.

Driver's cab

Metal shovel for pushing earth and stones

This bulldozer is clearing snow drifts so that people can ski down the mountain slopes safely.

Hovercraft

A hovercraft can move over land or on water. It floats on a large cushion of air.

Propellers push hovercraft forward

Rubber skirt

Air

Fan sucks in air

A large fan sucks air into the rubber skirt. The air lifts the hovercraft.

People travel across the sea in hovercraft. They can take their cars with them.

Doors open to let passengers drive on board

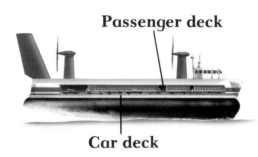

Passenger deck

Car deck

A hovercraft can carry as many as 400 people and 60 cars on one journey!

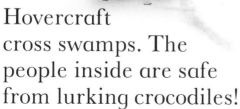

Hovercraft cross swamps. The people inside are safe from lurking crocodiles!

Crane

Cranes are powerful machines that can lift and move heavy loads.

Load

Cranes on building sites can be made taller as the building grows.

Dockyard cranes lift containers out of ships and load them onto trucks.

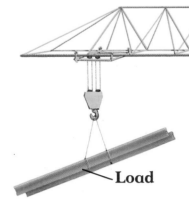

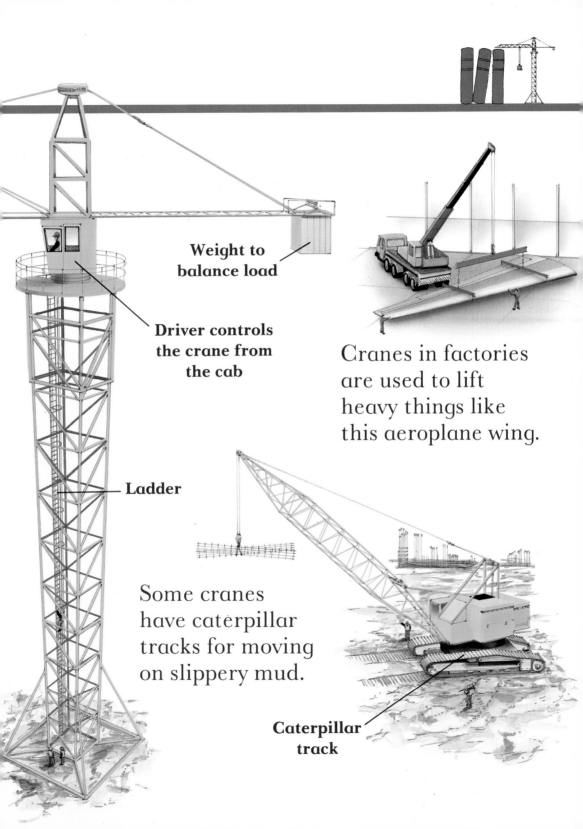

Weight to balance load

Driver controls the crane from the cab

Ladder

Cranes in factories are used to lift heavy things like this aeroplane wing.

Some cranes have caterpillar tracks for moving on slippery mud.

Caterpillar track

Jet aeroplane

Jet aeroplanes carry large numbers of people and goods very quickly from place to place.

Passenger cabins

Pilot's cabin

Executive jet

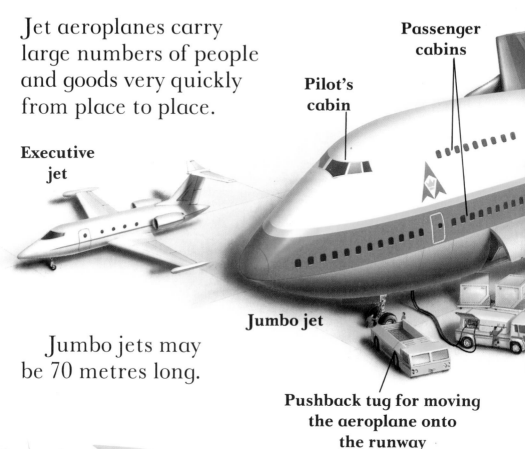

Jumbo jet

Jumbo jets may be 70 metres long.

Pushback tug for moving the aeroplane onto the runway

Cabin staff serve the passengers food and drink during the flight.

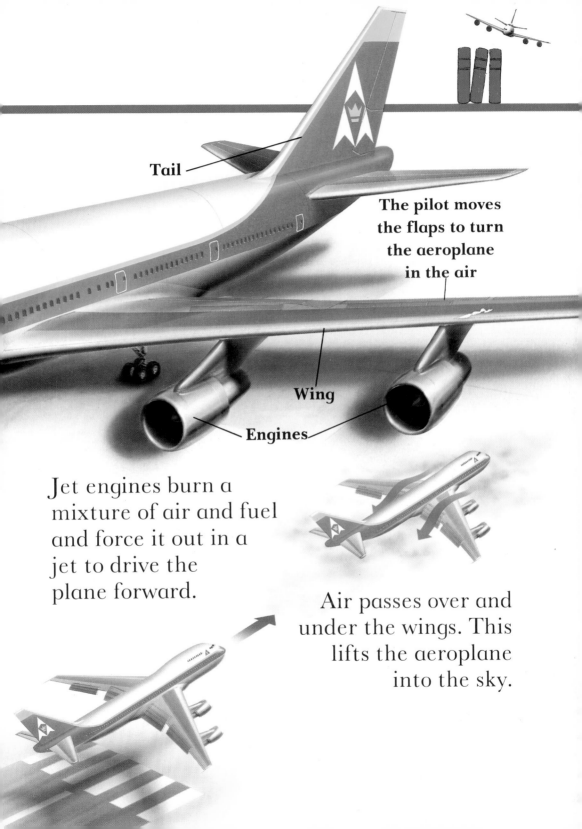

Tail

The pilot moves
the flaps to turn
the aeroplane
in the air

Wing

Engines

Jet engines burn a
mixture of air and fuel
and force it out in a
jet to drive the
plane forward.

Air passes over and
under the wings. This
lifts the aeroplane
into the sky.

Supertanker

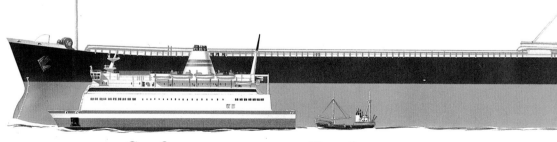

Car ferry

Trawler

Supertankers are huge ships. They can be more than 450 metres long.

Oil is carried in these huge tanks

Engines drive the supertanker

A supertanker is difficult to steer. It needs lots of room to turn and it takes 5 kilometres to stop!

Tugs pull the supertanker into the dock

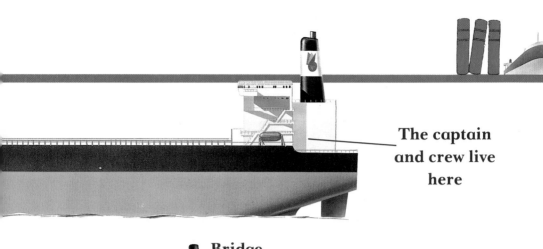

The captain and crew live here

Bridge

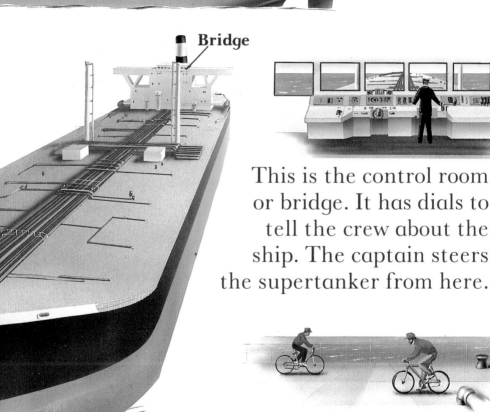

This is the control room or bridge. It has dials to tell the crew about the ship. The captain steers the supertanker from here.

The deck is so long that the crew have to ride around on bicycles.

Space shuttle

The space shuttle carries people called astronauts into orbit around Earth.

Powerful booster rockets fire the space shuttle into the sky.

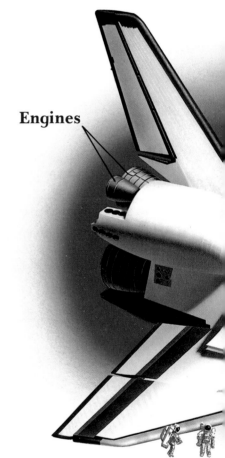

Engines

Booster rockets drop off in flight

Shuttle leaves launch pad

Astronauts wear space suits

Astronauts can climb outside the shuttle when they are in space.

Probes have no people inside

The astronauts release satellites and probes from the shuttle. They help us find out about planets and space.

Robot arm

Area where astronauts live and work

Payload bay holds cargo

Flight cabin

When the mission is over, the shuttle glides back down to Earth. It can be used again.

Submarine

Submarines are special types of ships that can dive deep beneath the surface of the sea.

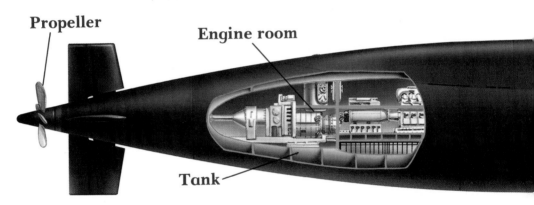

Propeller

Engine room

Tank

A submarine has tanks that fill with sea water to help it dive.

The submarine dives when the tanks fill with water

The submarine floats to the surface when the tanks empty

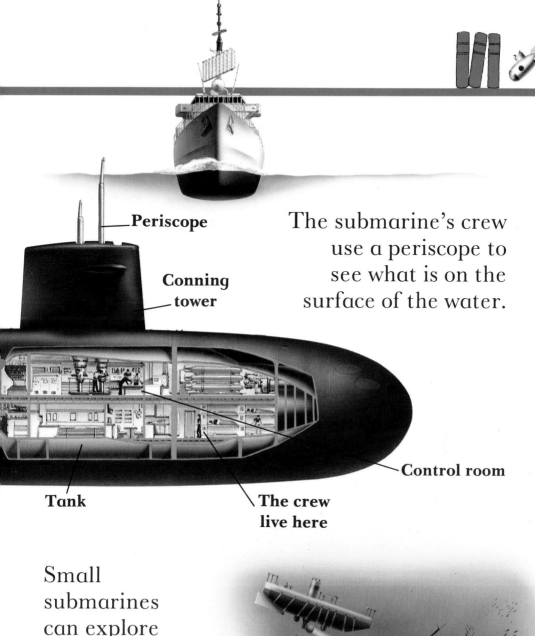

Periscope

Conning tower

The submarine's crew use a periscope to see what is on the surface of the water.

Control room

Tank

The crew live here

Small submarines can explore the bottom of the sea. Sometimes they find shipwrecks.

Truck

Trucks carry goods from place to place. Some trucks are more than 25 metres long.

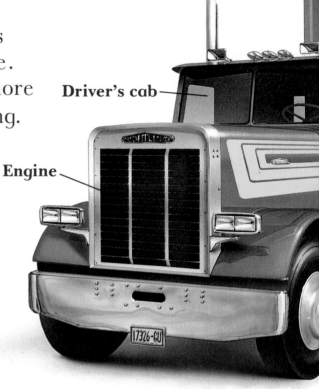

Driver's cab

Engine

Drivers can sleep overnight in their cab when they go on long journeys.

Bed

Seat folds down

You can see many types of truck on the road. Each type is built to carry different things.

Container is lifted off when truck arrives

This sign means that a truck is carrying dangerous chemicals. Watch out!

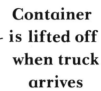

Animal transporter

Petrol tanker

Cement truck

Train

Trains are used to carry people and goods from place to place. They travel on rails made from steel.

Engine fuelled by diesel

Goods train

Engine

Some passenger trains have two engines so that they can change direction easily at the end of each journey.

Engine

**Boiler full
of steam**

The earliest
trains had steam engines.
You can still find steam
trains in some places.

**Tank
holds oil**

**Wagon
holds coal**

**Box wagon
holds food**

**Electricity passes
to engine from this cable**

This is the Japanese
"bullet train". It is an
extremely fast express
train. It can travel
256 kilometres
in one hour.

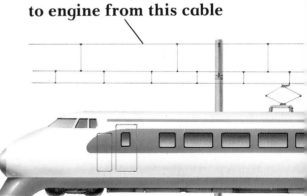

Can you remember?

How do bulldozers manage
to push earth?

What powers the engine
of this train?

What does the sign on the
back of this truck mean?

Which of these machines can
travel on both land and water?

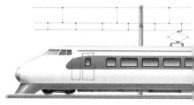